Meditations o

Stations
of the Cross

On the theme of forgiveness

FRAN GODFREY

McCrimmons
Great Wakering, Essex, England

First published in 2003 in the United Kingdom by
MCCRIMMON PUBLISHING CO. LTD.
10-12 High Street, Great Wakering, Essex SS3 0EQ
mccrimmons@dial.pipex.com
www.mccrimmons.com

ISBN 0 85597 645 4

Acknowledgements

We would like to thank Fr Michael O'Halloran S.J.
of Farm Street Church in London
for kindly allowing us to photograph the Stations there
and include them in this book.

Scripture quotations are taken from:
The Jerusalem Bible, published and copyright 1966, 1967 & 1968 and
The New Jerusalem Bible published and copyright 1985 by
Darton, Longman & Todd Ltd and Doubleday & Co. Inc.,
a division of Random House, and used by permission;
New American Bible with Revised Psalms © 1991, 1986, 1970
Confraternity of Christian Doctrine, Washington, D.C.
and are used with permission of the copyright owner. All rights reserved.
No part of the *New American Bible* may be reproduced in any form
without permission in writing from the copyright holder.

Every effort has been made to trace the owners of copyright material,
and we hope that no copyright has been infringed. Pardon is sought and apologies made
if the contrary be the case, and a correction will be made in any reprint of this book.

Cover design and layout by Nick Snode
Photography by Clive Austen, Kaz Studios, Essex
Typeset in 11 & 12pt Palatino roman and 24pt Aesop
Text pages printed on Fineblade Smooth 115gsm
Cover printed on 280gsm one sided art
Printed and bound by Thanet Press, Margate, Kent, England

Introduction

🙰 MY LORD,
 help me prepare to take these fourteen steps
  in memory of your Passion.
As each step led you closer to your death
 for love of me, so may I, with each step
 die more to myself.

Empty me, Beloved LORD,
 of all thoughts
 except those that will bring me to a deeper
  understanding
 of what you endured for my sake.

I offer myself
 and my small journey
 for all those who today still cause you agony
by perpetuating the rejection you suffered
 as God-made-Man.

May we never forget
 the depth of your love for us
 as you repeatedly forgive our sins
 which brought about your death.

LORD, if it is your will
 lay my cross on me gently
 and grant me the strength to carry it bravely
 with you and for love of you.

'"Let him who is without guilt cast the first stone..."

Jesus was left alone with the woman; he said,
"Where are they? Has no one condemned you?"
"No one, sir" she replied.
"Neither do I condemn you," said Jesus,
"Go, and sin no more."

'"Crucify him! Crucify him!". "Why?
What harm has this man done? I have found no case against
him that deserves death..." But they kept on shouting ...
...demanding he should be crucified ... Pilate handed Jesus
over to them to deal with as they pleased.'

First Station
Jesus is condemned to death

LORD, teach me
  not to judge nor harbour any unkind thoughts
    towards others.
I can understand so little
  and my judgement will almost always be biased
    by motives of jealousy, greed or pride.

Help me, instead, to recognise my own faults
  by allowing me to see myself as others see me,
  and – especially – as You see me –
and then grant me the strength
  to replace my shortcomings
    with meekness and generosity of spirit.

"Whoever wishes to come after me must deny himself,
take up his cross, and follow me."

Second Station
The Cross is laid on Jesus

TO DENY OURSELVES is to disown ourselves as the centre of our existence.

No matter how blessed we are in this life, we all have our crosses to bear. Nobody lives a life completely unmarked by pain or tribulation or sorrow or hardship – in mind or body. There is no escape from the cross. And Christ – fully human – bore the burden of His cross physically for all to see; to show that there is nothing He asks us to endure which He has not endured before us.

℘ LORD, teach me
    that to fight against accepting my cross
      adds immensely to its weight.
Show me how to lighten its load
    by accepting that it is the will of our Father
    that my life should have hardships,
for it is in the darkness of sorrow and pain
    that we seek most fervently the light of truth,
and in the chill of loneliness and despair
    that we struggle to draw close to the warm flame
    of your love for us.

"I tell you … there will be more joy in heaven over one sinner who repents than over ninety-nine righteous people who have no need of repentance."

"So I tell you, her many sins have been forgiven; hence, she has shown great love.
But the one to whom little is forgiven, loves little."

Third Station
Jesus falls the first time

THROUGHOUT HIS LIFE on earth, Our Lord tirelessly forgave sins, cured disease and disability – which had often plagued the sufferers all their lives. As we repeatedly stumble and fall from the same weaknesses we may have had for years, may we learn the lesson that God will never abandon us – unless we resolutely abandon Him.

℞ LORD,
    when you fell under the weight of your cross
        which bore my sins,
  you got up again and carried on –
        unswerving in your obedience to your Father.

Teach me to fix my sights on you,
    to persevere when I fall away from grace
    again and again.
Let me draw from the mercy you show me,
    the strength to defeat my weaknesses.

"I am the handmaid of the Lord," said Mary,
"let what you have said be done to me."

'"Simeon blessed them and said to Mary his mother,
"He is destined for the fall and rise of many in Israel,
destined to be a sign that is opposed – and a sword will
pierce your soul too ..."'

Fourth Station
Jesus meets his blessed mother

CAN THERE BE any more agonising pain than seeing the humiliation and indescribable suffering of the one you love most deeply, while being powerless to help?

⊱ MARY, Mother of God and of Man,
   help me to accept with serenity
      the hardships and struggles I must witness
      in the lives of those I care for and love.

Teach me to identify wisely
   when practical help is needed,
   when silent support is needed
and when my involvement would mean
   unwelcome interference.

*"They pressed into service a passer-by, Simon, a Cyrenian,
who was coming in from the country..."*

*"Jesus took Peter and James and John with him.
And a sudden fear came over him, and ... he said to them,
'My soul is sorrowful to the point of death. Wait here and
keep awake'... He came back and found them sleeping, and
he said to Peter, 'Simon, are you asleep? Had you not the
strength to keep awake one hour?'"*

Fifth Station
The Cross is laid upon Simon of Cyrene

THE TWO SIMONS: one a stranger who probably knew nothing
of Jesus; the other, one of Our Lord's closest and most ardent
friends. The stranger shouldered some of the weight of
Christ's cross; the friend didn't recognise the burden that
needed to be shared.

› LORD, it isn't always easy
    to see where help is needed.

Teach me that to concentrate on my own problems
    is to close my eyes to the often greater burdens
        of family, friends – and strangers.
May I learn to be less self-absorbed;
let me see how I may lighten the load of others –
    and thereby shoulder a tiny part of the weight
        of your cross.

"The soldiers twisted some thorns into a crown and put it on his head, and dressed him in a purple robe. They came up to him and said, 'Hail, king of the Jews!' and they slapped him in the face … Jesus then came out wearing the crown of thorns and the purple robe. Pilate said: 'Ecce Homo.'"

"As Jesus prayed, the aspect of his face was changed and his clothing became brilliant as lightning. … 'This is my Son, the Chosen One. Listen to him.'"

Sixth Station
Veronica wipes the face of Jesus

WHAT MOVED VERONICA to come forward from the surging
masses and risk rough treatment from the brutal soldiers
trying to control the frenzied crowd? Was it pure compassion
at the sight of the bleeding, bruised face of Jesus? Or did she
see something of the Chosen One in this scourged and
bloodied figure? Did she feel the desperate need to make
contact with the man whose touch had healed so many?

☙ LORD, teach me
    that even when I feel afraid and helpless
    to ease the burdens of others,
the smallest gesture can mean a lot.
Sometimes just a smile or a kind word
    or a touch of the hand can make a difference.
May I treat kindly everyone I meet –
    not just the attractive and appealing people
      who are easy to be near.

"While he was still a long way off, his father saw him and was moved with pity. He ran to the boy, clasped him in his arms and kissed him.

'This son of mine was dead and has come back to life; he was lost and is found.'"

Seventh Station
Jesus falls the second time

CHRIST THE MAN, exhausted and aching in every limb and sinew, falls a second time, but again gets up and struggles on.

To fall is human; to get up again we need divine help.

God will always welcome back the sinner who, having fallen, overcomes his pride, recognises his total dependence on his Creator and reaches out for the help and strength of forgiveness.

LORD,
   take my hand in yours, help me up.
   I know that if I manage even one small faltering step
      towards you, in your great love
      you will come out to meet me.

"Jesus turned to them and said,
'Daughters of Jerusalem, do not weep for me;
weep instead for yourselves and for your children.'"

Eighth Station
The women of Jerusalem mourn for Jesus

HOW HARD IT MUST HAVE BEEN to look on the flogged and
bleeding figure of Jesus as He struggled under the weight of
his cross, and not weep. Yet Our Lord was not moved by self-
pity, but pity for the suffering destined for His people; pity for
the sufferings Man would inflict upon Man.

Today it is all too easy to weep for ourselves, blurring our
sight of how the wrongs we have done have brought pain and
disappointment to our loving Father.

❧ LORD, teach us
to turn our tears of self-pity into tears of shame
for the agony we have caused you;
lead us to make positive changes in ourselves
to remove those things which hurt you,
so that our tears may be turned to joy
as we feel your presence in our souls
and in our lives.

"Then Peter approaching asked him, 'Lord, if my brother sins against me, how often must I forgive him? As many as seven times?'

Jesus answered, 'I say to you not seven times, but seventy-seven times.'"

Ninth Station
Jesus falls the third time

AT THE THIRD FALL surely it is nearly all over.
Surely Our Lord cannot drag himself up again. And yet he
does. Do we? As we repeatedly fall, aren't we ready to give
up? Utterly defeated, dejected and despairing of ourselves
and our right to any forgiveness at all. Yet Jesus taught us that
there is no end to the Father's mercy as long as we keep on
trying, keep on turning to Him for help.

When Christ created His Church, He left us what we need to
be saved: "Whose sins you forgive, they are forgiven."

   LORD, teach us
      to respect and rejoice in the sacraments
         you left your Church –
   the continuous opportunities for forgiveness and
         spiritual nourishment.
   May we never become complacent or cavalier
         in our attitude to the means of our salvation,
   but gain an ever greater understanding
         of your boundless mercy.

" ...the soldiers... took his clothing and divided it into four
shares, one for each soldier. His undergarment was seamless...
so they said to one another, 'Instead of tearing it, let's throw
dice to decide who is to have it.'"

Tenth Station
Jesus is stripped of His garments

THE FINAL INDIGNITY – to stand naked before a jeering rabble.
Stared at by eyes that were too blind to see the Truth.

The callousness of the soldiers defies belief as they share out
Our Lord's clothes; showing more interest in throwing dice for
them, than in the man who was about to die the most
agonising death - out of love for them.

Killing some time – as they killed their Saviour.

ℂ➤ BELOVED LORD,
 I know that I am always naked before you.
 Nothing I do escapes your notice;
 I need never bother to offer excuses or explanations
  for anything I do – or don't do.
 You see me as I am,
  and you see the potential you created in me.
 Please clear my mind of trivia
  and help me to become the person
   you want me to be,
 rather than a worthless shell
  wrapped in earthly trappings.

"Father forgive them;
they know not what they do."

Eleventh Station
Jesus is nailed to the Cross

FOR ALL THE PAIN we have caused Him, still His love makes excuses for us.

The cross on which Christ hung is the most powerful image in the history of mankind. The simplicity of two pieces of wood belying the complexity of its meaning for us. To gaze on it is to the see the pain, the burdens, the rejection, the injustice which Our Lord bore for love of us ; it's to see the ultimate sacrifice; it's to see the Way, the Truth – and the hope of glorious, eternal life.

But to earn a share in Christ's glory we must also endure a share of His suffering. We who are the cause of it.

℞ LORD, teach us
  to be brave;
  to accept without complaint the pains
    and hardships which may come our way.
Not to question why, but to say always:

Let thy will, not mine, be done.

To accept your will is to receive your grace.

"Jesus, remember me when you come into your kingdom."
"Indeed I promise you … today you will be with me in paradise."

"Father, into your hands I commend my spirit."

"In truth, this Man was a son of God."

Twelfth Station
Jesus Dies on the Cross

IT IS ALL OVER. There must be some relief as the agony stops, the taunts die away; the body of Our Lord feels, sees, hears no more as His life drains away with His blood. The Son of God has accomplished His Father's will.

To those at the foot of the cross this must have been the bleakest hour. How would they manage? Why should they even bother? What had it all been for?

The Mystery of the Cross.

℣ LORD,
     we know that your death was not the end,
     but the means by which we can reach our end –
       our goal.
   You died before us to show us
     that obedience to the Father's will
      and dying to ourselves
       is the way to Life.

As those we love reach the end of their lives
   on earth,
grant that they may soon join you in perfect peace
   and happiness
and grant us the consolation
   which comes from faith and trust in Your mercy.

"When they came to Jesus they found that he was already dead, and so instead of breaking his legs, one of the soldiers pierced his side with a lance; and immediately there came out blood and water.

This is the evidence of one who saw it."

Thirteenth Station
Jesus is taken down from the Cross

AGAIN OUR THOUGHTS turn to the beloved disciple John, to Mary and the other women who loved Jesus. What was there to say? What words of consolation could they offer one another as they tenderly took the bruised, lifeless corpse down from the cross. Mary, there to the end, bravely hugs the marble-cold body of her Son to herself, as her friends gently prise Him from her arms. It is over; He has gone. A sword pierced her soul.

☜ LORD,
>   sometimes it is hard, sometimes impossible,
>   to see why things happen.
>   Tragic, heart-breaking things happen to
>   good people, to children, to the vulnerable –
>   and the world asks 'why?'
>
>   Help us to learn
>   how to accept what we don't understand
>   and to trust, to be still
>   and know that God is always near.
>
>   Banish the pride which dictates to us
>   that we have a right to know everything.
>   Console us in our grief
>   and save us from despair.

"Joseph took the body, wrapped it in a clean shroud
and put it in his own new tomb
which he had hewn out of the rock.
He then rolled a large stone across the entrance of the tomb
and went away."

Fourteenth Station
Jesus is laid in the Sepulchre

JOSEPH OF ARIMATHAEA was described as a prominent member of the Council, a virtuous and upright man who had not agreed with what the others had planned and carried out. His voice was a lone voice, drowned out by the noisy majority. Still he made his views known and having failed to prevent the atrocity, bravely went to Pilate and asked for the body of Jesus. He then carefully wrapped the body, and laid it in a new tomb which he had prepared for his own use.

LORD,
  there will be times when I will have to stand up
    against the majority,
speak out against the popular principles
    of an immoral society
    which has rejected the notion of self-denial
    and lives only for self-gratification.

It might not be easy to stand out from the crowd,
    it might make no difference to anyone,
but may I never deny what I have learned to be true
    from trying to follow your teaching,
    and your Way of the Cross.

31

Simon Peter ... went into the tomb, saw the linen cloths lying on the ground and also the cloth that had been over his head; this was not with the linen cloths but rolled up in a place by itself. Then the other disciple ... also went in; he saw and he believed."

"Come to me all you who are overburdened and I will give you rest."

"I am the resurrection and the life. If anyone believes in me, even though he dies he will live, and whoever lives and believes in me will never die."

Fifteenth Station
The Resurrection

WHAT WERE THE INITIAL THOUGHTS going through the heads of John and Peter? After all the anguish of the previous days, the humiliation of Christ's death on the Cross, they could be forgiven for being confused when confronted with the empty tomb; for not remembering that their beloved Lord had promised he would rise again after three days. It was John, the disciple loved especially by the Lord, who saw, understood and believed first what the others came also to believe.

❧ LORD, at times it is hard to keep my faith
burning ever brightly.
Sometimes the flame of my belief grows dim,
especially, when I am confronted by the enormity
of my sinfulness
or by the pains and sorrows of this life.
When I struggle with my small crosses,
when I am tempted to ask 'why me?'
help me to remember that in my suffering
I share in yours.
I trust in your promise that I may also share
in your resurrection to supreme happiness
in your presence for all eternity.

MY LORD,
be always with me in this life,
so that I may be with you in the next.

Final Prayer

❧ My LORD, My GOD, My ALL –

the deep sadness and shame I feel
    as I have tried to imagine some of what you
        suffered for me,
is softened by a gratitude I can never express,
an unfaltering hope in your infinite mercy and
an immovable trust in your undying love.

Possess me, LORD;
flood the darkness of my sinful being
    with the light of your grace
until there is nothing in my thoughts,
    words or deeds which can ever offend or
        disappoint you again.

LORD, with the words "Thy will be done" –
I willingly accept my cross,
trusting that your love means I shall never be left
    to carry it alone.

Amen.

SCRIPTURAL REFERENCES

1st Station	John 8:7-11
2nd Station	Matthew 16:24
3rd Station	Luke 15:7, Luke 7:47
4th Station	Luke 1:38, Luke 2:33
5th Station	Mark 15:21, Mark 14:32/37
6th Station	John 19:1-3 and 14, Luke 9:28 and 35
7th Station	Luke 15:20 and 24
8th Station	Luke 23:27
9th Station	Matthew 18:21
10th Station	John 19:23-24
11th Station	Luke 23:34
12th Station	Luke 23:42/43, 46, 47
13th Station	John 19:33-34
14th Station	Matthew 27:59-60
15th Station	John 20:6-8, Matthew 11:28, John 11:25

Biography

Fran was born in London. Her family lived for a few years in Southern Rhodesia (Zimbabwe), then Oxford, before settling in a village on the south coast near Bournemouth.

Convent-educated Fran trained as a bi-lingual secretary, before changing tack completely and joining the local radio station in Dorset where she worked as a technical operator, commercial producer and presenter for 7 years.

In 1990 Fran joined BBC Radio 2 as a newsreader/announcer – and butt of Terry Wogan's relentless teasing, for which she has been well-prepared by having two brothers and a witty punster as a father!

A 'cradle-Catholic', Fran can nevertheless date the growth in, and transformation of, her faith from the time she joined the parish of St James's in Spanish Place, London where she met the wise, funny, clever and deeply devout Mgr. Frederick Miles, to whom she feels indebted for her spiritual awakening.

Fran lives with her laptop computer in 'a tiny flat' in central London!